The HOW-TO's of Life!

How to Make and Keep FRIENDS!

featuring

Illustrated by Cecilia Coto

MEET THE CHARACTERS!

Sophie, a pink elephant, is very kind but extremely shy. She is often afraid of new situations and finds meeting new people difficult. Sophie is insecure about her unique, pink appearance.

Sparkelina®, a young girl, is the wisest of the group. She has spent many years observing children and is a patient and loving mentor to her friends Busybee and Sophie.

Busybee, a giant bee, is goodhearted, energetic, and impulsive. As a bee, he is used to flying freely from place to place and has a hard time understanding etiquette and rules.

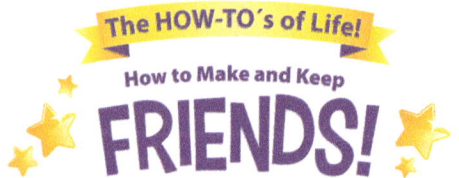

Original Title: How to Make and Keep Friends!

Text: Kinderwise®
First Edition, March 2016

Illustrations: Cecilia Coto
Printed in U.S.A.

Copyright © 2016 by Kinderwise®
ALL RIGHTS RESERVED.

ISBN 978-0-9972413-3-4

All rights reserved. No part of this publication, including but not limited to the content, illustrations, and names such as Sparkelina and Kinderwise may be reproduced, stored in a retrieval system, or transmitted in any form or by any means, electronic, mechanical, photocopying, recording or otherwise, without the prior written permission of the publisher. Unauthorized use or reproduction of any aspect of this publication is strictly prohibited and may result in legal action. For permissions, email creator and publisher at kinderwise@gmail.com.

SUGGESTED READING METHODS:

1. Ask your child what each character is feeling and why.

2. Have any of these situations ever happened to you or your child? What did you do?

3. Can your child think of another way to deal with each situation?

4. Each negative is paired with a positive solution (left to right on the pages). Cover the right page and ask your child what they think the character should do before revealing the answer.

5. Ask if your child knows anyone in the neighborhood or at school that has acted in any of the ways portrayed in the book. What happened and what could have been done differently?

6. All the characters in the book are kind but sometimes don't think about the consequences of their actions. Ask your child to name a GOOD quality about any person you may have discussed while reading this book and how that might make them a good friend.

These are just suggestions. Be creative with your topics!

Hands can sometimes hurt.

Las manos a veces pueden lastimar.

Use them to hug your friends.

Úsalas para abrazar a tus amigos.

Keeping toys to yourself means you'll play alone.

Guardar los juguetes para ti mismo significa que juegas solo.

Share and be a friend.

Comparte y se un amigo.

Being shy is okay.

Ser tímido está bien.

Try saying, "Hello."

Trata de decir, "Hola."

Mouths are not for biting.

Las bocas no son para morder.

Use your words.

Usa tus palabras.

Playing with others means joining in.

Jugar con otros significa unirse.

Find something everyone wants to play.

Encuentra algo que todos quieran jugar.

Laughing at someone is unkind.

Reírse de alguien es grosero.

Help your friends.

Ayuda a tus amigos.

Honesty can sometimes be hard.

La honestidad a veces puede ser difícil.

This is when trust grows the most.

Esto es cuando la confianza crece más.

A good friend thinks of others.

Un buen amigo piensa en otros.

Always take turns.

Siempre tomen turnos.

Telling friends they are wrong

isn't fun for them.

Decirles a los amigos que están equivocados
no es divertido para ellos.

Playing differently is okay, too.

Jugar de manera diferente está bien también.

When accidents happen...

Cuando los accidentes pasan...

...remember to say, "I'm sorry."

...recuerda decir, "Lo siento."

Don't get upset when your pal plays with others.

No te molestes cuando tu amigo juega con otros.

It's okay to have more than one friend.

Está bien tener más de un amigo.

Sometimes friends say no.

A veces los amigos dicen no.

This is ok. Find something else to do.

Esto está bien. Encuentra algo más que hacer.

Jealousy is not friendship.

Los celos no son amistad.

Be happy when others succeed.

You can, too.

Se feliz cuando otros triunfan. Tu puedes también.

Leaving someone out will make them sad.

Dejar a alguien fuera lo hace sentir mal.

Include all your friends.

Incluye a todos tus amigos.

ABOUT KINDERWISE®

Kinderwise® and characters were founded by a dedicated mother based in Southern California who recognized the importance of teaching children essential life skills in a memorable way. With a focus on emotional intelligence, she created an acclaimed book series entitled "Emotional Intelligence Program for Children" and other educational products "The HOW-TO's of LIFE" featuring her beloved characters Sparkelina® (a young girl), Busybee (a giant bee), and Sophie (a pink elephant). Together, these characters navigate the challenges of the world, learning valuable lessons in a delightful and engaging manner. Kinderwise® and characters aim to provide children with a fun and interactive learning experience, fostering personal growth and development.

Why an emotional intelligence book series? The desire for a clear, accessible approach to emotional intelligence development stemmed from the personal experience of the female founder of Kinderwise®. Raised by an orphaned mother with Asperger syndrome and a highly intelligent, yet anti-social father, she found childhood social interaction to be a challenge. She read book after book to "fill in the blanks" of her own lack of social knowledge. She discovered that empathy, awareness of feelings, self-regulation and people skills form the foundation for a successful, happy life.

This guide can be used to re-enforce the daily life lessons that the founder taught her own son. She felt it was important that the book be written from the perspective of a child. To do this, she created three imaginary friends. Much like children, these characters would have to learn how to get along with each other and others. *The How-To's of Life!* book series was born.

Your support helps Kinderwise® to continue creating educational books and products aimed at helping children develop essential social skills. For more information, email: kinderwise@gmail.com